THE LITTLE GUIDE TO
WILDFLOWERS

THE LITTLE GUIDE TO
WILDFLOWERS

Illustrations
by Tom Frost

Words by
Alison Davies

Hardie Grant

QUADRILLE

Introduction

What makes a flower wild? Is it the ability to thrive against the odds, to withstand the elements or take root in the strangest places? Tenacity is surely a part of what makes these often tender-looking shrubs so special, for they adapt and make their home wherever they can. Perhaps it is their unique beauty, the array of colours and shapes, the daubed and patterned leaves, and sometimes the burst of fragrance that accompanies their presence. Or maybe it is something otherworldly, a gift hidden deep within the petal folds, the purest golden nectar, or a remedy of old that we can still apply today. There are so many facets to these beautiful blooms that often get overlooked, but here within these pages they are celebrated, captured in amazing artistry, and brought to life. The stories and facts that make them special are highlighted, along with all the information you will need to get out into the wild and see them for yourself.

You'll learn about their uses and how they grow, you'll also discover the secrets behind their glory, and in doing so will understand the importance of each and every floral beauty. From woodland wonders, such as Bluebells and Snowdrops, to medicinal miracles such as Red Clover and Winter Cress – then there are the folklore favourites that exude an air of mystery: herbs like Yarrow, with its wildly witchy connotations and a history for the arcane. Even Dandelions, often considered the gardener's pest, take their rightful place, being key pollinators and tellers of time.

Whatever you are looking for, you will find it here.

Open the pages of this book and breathe in the sweet scent of each flower, appreciate its individual essence, and experience the joy of wildflowers from around the world.

'If all flowers wanted to be roses, nature would lose her springtime beauty and the fields would no longer be decked out with little wildflowers.'

THÉRÈSE OF LISIEUX

Blue Iris

Iris spuria

FAMILY NAME Iridaceae

CHARACTERISTICS A rhizomatous perennial with sword-like leaves that rise from a basal cluster with violet blue flowers

HABITAT Damp grasslands, meadows, marshes, swamps and bogs

DISTRIBUTION Found in Europe, Asia and Africa

FLOWERS AND FRUIT Vibrantly veined violet blooms with yellow sepals; flowers late spring to early summer

This elegant bloom grows to 91.4 152.5 cm (3–5 ft) high, making it one of the tallest in its family. A favourite of bees and other pollinators, it has a strong stem that holds aloft the beautiful flowers. Legend suggests it gets its name from the Greek Goddess of the rainbow, Iris. Her colourful rainbow bridge connected earth with the heavenly realm, making her a messenger to the deities. As such the flowers are seen as a symbol of faith and hope.

Rock Rose

Cistus

FAMILY NAME Cistaceae

CHARACTERISTICS A bushy evergreen shrub that can grow between 50.8 cm (20 in) and 1.8 m (6 ft) tall; it has silvery grey green leaves and white, pink or reddish blooms

HABITAT Stony ground, gravel and coastal gardens

DISTRIBUTION Found in temperate areas of Europe, the Mediterranean and North America

FLOWERS AND FRUIT The papery thin flowers have three or five petals and come in a range of shades; the fruit is a capsule with five or ten valves

These fragile blooms are short lived but incredibly sweet scented, thanks to the essential oils they secrete. The compounds in the oils are highly antioxidant, particularly when used to fight bacterial and fungus infections. The leaves, too, are aromatic, and often covered in a sticky resin. Not to be confused with the Helianthemum, a beautiful alpine flower that shares the *Cistus* mantle, this type of Rock Rose thrives in drought tolerant landscapes.

Cornflower

Centaurea cyanus

FAMILY NAME Asteraceae

CHARACTERISTICS A multi-stemmed plant, between 30.5–91.4 cm (12–36 in) in height; it has blue grey leaves and vibrant blue flowers

HABITAT Grain fields, cornfields, fallow land, roadsides and waste ground; a popular choice today for gardens

DISTRIBUTION Native to Europe, cultivated in North America where it has naturalised as an invasive species

FLOWERS AND FRUIT Blooms from late spring through to autumn

Also known as the Bachelor's Button, Cornflower is a herb that originally thrived in cornfields and has since become a prized ornamental bloom. A symbol of wealth, fertility and love, the flower was often worn in a man's lapel to signal his single status to the woman of his choosing. If the flower wilted fast, then this showed the woman's interest had also waned. Young maidens chose to wear this bloom to show potential suitors that they were available for marriage. With its spicy, clove-like flavour it is often made into tea, which has the added benefit of reducing congestion and fever.

Italian Buckthorn

Rhamnus alaternus

FAMILY NAME Rhamnaceae

CHARACTERISTICS This large shrub can grow up to 4.9 m (16 ft) high, with alternating leaves and tiny green flowers clustered in the leaf forks

HABITAT Grasslands, open woodlands, coastal environs, waste ground and roadsides

DISTRIBUTION Native to Europe and western Asia

FLOWERS AND FRUIT Flowers are green to yellow in hue and fused at the base, they usually have four to five petals; it has small berry-like fruit, which contain three nutlets

Widely cultivated as an ornamental garden or hedging plant, Italian Buckthorn is prized for its sweetly fragrant flowers, which appear from late spring to mid-autumn. With glossy dark green leaves it's an eye-catching evergreen, with berries that change colour from green to red and then to blackish brown as they fully mature. Also known as the Blow Fly Bush and the Evergreen Buckthorn, it's often seen as a threat to biodiversity, because it is fast growing and easily dominates other vegetation.

Common Daisy

Bellis perennis

FAMILY NAME Asteraceae

CHARACTERISTICS A herbaceous plant with creeping roots and spoon-shaped leaves, which form a rosette at the base and can be smooth or covered in hairs

HABITAT Grasslands, meadows, urban areas and gardens

DISTRIBUTION Worldwide, except in Antarctica

FLOWERS AND FRUIT Flowers have a yellow button-like disc and a fan surround of white petals, usually blooms late spring to early summer

The hardy Daisy can be seen in abundance in the wild, as it easily conquers new habitats and is impervious to most pesticides. This pretty flower is related to the Artichoke and recognised as a symbol of purity around the world. The name comes from the Anglo Saxon word *daes eage*, which means 'day's eyes', and is a nod to the fact that the Daisy opens its petals at dawn and closes them at dusk. Rich in vitamin C, this humble bloom can be used in cooking and salads and has been cultivated since Roman times for its healing properties.

Cowslip

Primula veris

FAMILY NAME Primulaceae

CHARACTERISTICS A perennial that has oval leaves with wrinkled edges, and cup-shaped yellow flowers

HABITAT Open fields, pastures, roadside verges, gardens and grasslands

DISTRIBUTION Cowslips are native to Europe, Algeria and western Asia

FLOWERS AND FRUIT Deep yellow blooms that grow in clusters on tall stalks, flowers in spring and summer; the fruit capsule is around 1.9 cm (¾ in) in length

Often confused with the Primrose (see page 70), this golden bloom is a common sight in meadows and was traditionally picked on May Day and used as a decorative addition to garlands and wreaths. It's also known as St Peter's Keys because of the key-like shape of the one-sided flower heads. In folk medicine the plant was used to induce sleep thanks to its sedative qualities. Originally christened with the less genteel title Cowslop, as it grew in abundance near cow pats, the name has evolved into the more appealing Cowslip over time.

Meadow Saxifrage

Saxifraga granulata

FAMILY NAME Saxifragaceae

CHARACTERISTICS A clump-forming perennial, long stalked, with dark green kidney-shaped leaves and white blooms

HABITAT Grassland habitats including pastures, roadside verges, churchyards and flood meadows

DISTRIBUTION Widespread through Northern, Western and central Europe

FLOWERS AND FRUIT Delicate snowy white flowers usually appear mid-spring

This plant can sometimes be hard to spot because of the way the leaves smother the ground; being low to the earth, they remain a vivid deep green during the winter months. The five petalled flowers are an elegant addition to borders and roadsides. The Romans believed that these delightful blooms were more than just pleasing to the eye. Observing the way they would grow in rocky crevices, they coined the name *Saxifraga* meaning 'stone breaking'. Their ability to split rock is highly unlikely but these pretty plants are in decline, thanks to a lack of its natural habitat.

Creeping Buttercup

Ranunculus repens

FAMILY NAME Ranunculaceae

CHARACTERISTICS Has runners that spread over large areas; the hairy leaves have three lobes and the golden flowers are cup shaped

HABITAT Damp grassy places such as meadows, pastures, woodland, fields and gardens

DISTRIBUTION Widespread throughout Britain and most of Europe, also native to North Africa and Asia

FLOWERS AND FRUIT Bright yellow, glossy flowers with at least five petals, buttercups reproduce by seed and have long stolons that start growing in the spring

This low-growing, creeping perennial is a golden feast for the eye. The beautifully-crafted cups have delighted generations as they shed a gold light when placed under the chin. A common belief was that swallows fed their young with the flowers to give them the gift of prophecy. Another folk tale suggests that Buttercups are the product of fairy magic; a group of mischievous sprites happened upon a miser carrying a bag of treasure, so they cut a hole in the bottom to leave a trail of gold nuggets in the grass. They quickly transformed this bounty into flowers.

Bluebell

Hyacinthoides

FAMILY NAME Asparagaceae

CHARACTERISTICS A perennial herb with bright violet-blue bell
shaped flowers

HABITAT Shady spots, in woodland, hedgerows and fields

DISTRIBUTION Native to Western Europe

FLOWERS AND FRUIT Flowers have six petals and up-turned lips;
they droop to one side of the stem and have white coloured pollen inside

Enter an ancient woodland in the spring, and you're sure to find
a carpet of Bluebells at your feet. The glorious swathe of colour,
coupled with a sweet aroma, adds to the air of mystery so it's no
wonder this flower is synonymous with magic, a favourite of the
fey and a place where fairies gather. According to the folklore
should you dare to pick a Bluebell in the wild then you'll find
yourself wandering the fairy otherworld for eternity. A symbol of
everlasting love and humility, the Bluebell provides succour for a
variety of pollinators, including butterflies, bees and hoverflies.

25

Yarrow

Achillea millefolium

FAMILY NAME Asteraceae

CHARACTERISTICS A hardy perennial that grows up to 91.4 cm (36 in) in height; it has clusters of white flowers and feathery, fern-like leaves

HABITAT Grasslands, lawns, meadows, waste ground

DISTRIBUTION Found throughout North America from the coast to the alpine zone, and in Europe and Asia

FLOWERS AND FRUIT It has small white flattened flowers that bloom late summer; the fruit, known as an achene, is oblong in shape and contains a single seed

Yarrow is a member of the Daisy family and has tiny ray-shaped flowers that grow in delicate frothy white clusters. Popular in ancient times because of its healing powers, it was commonly used in poultices and ointments to treat wounds, particularly on the battlefield. Often called the Devil's Nettle, it does have a reputation for the arcane and was a favourite ingredient in spells to divine the future. According to medieval folklore, a dried bundle of this herb was the perfect wedding gift. If hung over the newlywed's bed it would ensure that their love endured for seven years.

Dandelion

Taraxacum

FAMILY NAME Asteraceae

CHARACTERISTICS Has a rosette of leaves at the base of the plant and
a hollow stem; the bloom presents a bright yellow head with ray flowers

HABITAT Grasslands, from lawns to meadows and roadside verges

DISTRIBUTION Native to Europe and Asia, but found all over the world

FLOWERS AND FRUIT Yellow flowers that turn into silvery white tufted
heads; these fruits disperse in the wind to propagate widely

The common Dandelion may be the gardener's nemesis, but in full
bloom it's a golden delight, carpeting grassy meadows in sunshine.
When the seed head, also known as a 'clock', appears, the vista
is transformed into a sea of fluffy whiteness. A key food source
for pollinators, this controversial bloom is the subject of folklore
around the world. Used as a tool for divination, some beliefs suggest
that if you blow away all of the seeds in one breath, then your love
is requited. In other traditions, the number of seeds left on the
'clock' denote the number of children you will have.

29

Common Dog Violet

Viola riviniana

FAMILY NAME Violaceae

CHARACTERISTICS This pretty plant has long-stalked heart-shaped leaves and bright violet to blue flowers

HABITAT Woods, hedge banks, pastures, along country lanes, road verges, moorland

DISTRIBUTION Native to Eurasia and Africa, common throughout the British Isles

FLOWERS AND FRUIT These blooms have five petals backed by small pointed sepals and an upturned flower spur, which is paler than the petals

Being scentless these springtime beauties were only considered fit for dogs, hence their name. While they may not have the fragrance of Sweet Violets they are just as lovely to behold, and spread rapidly, as their stolons run above the ground. They're a sanctuary for rare butterflies like the Silver-washed Fritillary and the High Brown Fritillary, who feast on them and use them as a safe haven for their eggs. The Ancient Greeks believed these gorgeous blooms to be a symbol of romance.

30

Solomon's Seal

Polygonatum

FAMILY NAME Asparagaceae

CHARACTERISTICS A herbaceous perennial with ribbed foliage and arched stems that have white bell-shaped blooms hanging beneath

HABITAT Woodlands edges, fence rows, roadsides

DISTRIBUTION Native to Asia, Europe and North America

FLOWERS AND FRUIT Tubular creamy white flowers that appear in late spring and transform into black or red berries in the autumn

Gently curving and graceful, this plant gets its name from the indentation left by the stem after it breaks away from the root. Believed to resemble the seal of Solomon, a symbol on a signet ring belonging to the King, it was thought to control demons and genies. It's no surprise then that this wildflower has mystical connotations. In folk magic it's used to protect against evil spirits. The 'seal' part of the title also relates to the plant's curative capacity, for sealing wounds and healing broken bones.

33

Red Campion

Silene dioica

FAMILY NAME Caryophyllaceae

CHARACTERISTICS A hairy perennial growing to around 97.5 cm (38 in) in height, it has pink flowers with five split petals

HABITAT Woodland, grassland, hedge rows, roadside verges and rocky ground

DISTRIBUTION Native throughout Europe, it has been introduced to other countries such as Iceland, Canada, the US and Argentina

FLOWERS AND FRUIT The petals of the flower are fused at the base to form a tube; the fruit is a capsule with ten teeth enclosed by a large tubular calyx

According to folklore Red Campion has protective properties and is commonly found guarding honeybee stores and fairy dwellings. Its family name *silene* comes from the Greek word *sialon*, which means saliva; this relates to the sticky substance the plant secretes from its stem. Used in traditional remedies to soothe snake bites, Red Campion is not just a pretty addition to a patch of woodland – it's also a favourite of pollinating insects like bees and butterflies.

Yellow Wort

Blackstonia perfoliata

FAMILY NAME Gentianaceae

CHARACTERISTICS A flowering herb with pointed blueish green leaves in pairs, positioned together upon the stem; the flower is yellow

HABITAT Chalk and limestone grasslands, and on sand dunes

DISTRIBUTION Found around the Mediterranean basin and extending into northwest Europe

FLOWERS AND FRUIT Blooms from summer to mid-autumn, the flowers resemble buttercups, with six to eight petals; the fruit is a rounded capsule

The waxy leaves of this plant, which sit opposite each other and look like they are unified, help it to thrive by retaining water. The beautiful blooms also respond to the environment, opening early in the morning to soak up the sun and then closing mid-afternoon, or when the sun slips behind a cloud. While this wildflower favours chalky grasslands, it can also grow at roadsides, by paths and railways, and in quarries.

Red Clover

Trifolium pratense

FAMILY NAME Fabaceae

CHARACTERISTICS This perennial evergreen has rose-coloured flowers, with hollow, hairy stems and leaves that are palmately trifoliolate

HABITAT Grasslands, including pasture, meadows, lawns, waste ground, forest margins and roadsides

DISTRIBUTION Has a worldwide distribution and is native to Europe, Western Asia and Northwest Africa

FLOWERS AND FRUIT Blooms from spring to early autumn, with rounded clusters of pinkish red flowers; the fruit is an indehiscent pod inside the calyx

This herbaceous plant is part of the bean family and grows in abundance throughout the world; because of this it's often used as fodder for livestock. While it might be a favourite for grazing animals, it's also of benefit to humans and can be used in teas and other tinctures and preparations to soothe a fever, loosen mucus and also as a diuretic. To the ancients, this three-leaved herb was sacred, and associated with the triple goddess of Greek and Roman myth. Druids believed that it could ward off evil spells and curses.

Autumn Crocus

Colchicum autumnale

FAMILY NAME Colchicaceae

CHARACTERISTICS A perennial herb with basal, slender leaves and tubular flowers ranging from purplish pink to white

HABITAT Grasslands, meadows, open woodland, roadside verges

DISTRIBUTION Native to Europe and North Africa

FLOWERS AND FRUIT Long, goblet-shaped flowers, with golden stamens; the blooms are wide at the top and slender at the base

While this graceful bloom brings much delight, it also heralds the coming of winter. With its soft petalled beauty, it's a popular and pretty addition to any autumn scene. Also known as Naked Ladies because the flowers appear long before the wrinkly green leaves, which usually emerge in spring and can stifle more delicate plants. The leaves will then wither away in time for the flowers to take centre stage. Highly toxic to grazing and domestic animals, the Autumn Crocus is actually a form of Meadow Saffron.

Yellow Archangel

Lamium galeobdolon

FAMILY NAME Lamiaceae

CHARACTERISTICS A hairy perennial, with grooved heart-shaped or oval leaves and yellow hooded flowers

HABITAT Woodland floors and hedgerows

DISTRIBUTION Widespread throughout Europe and western Asia

FLOWERS AND FRUIT Flowers are in whorls of four to ten along the upper half of the stem; the fruit can be found in the calyx, which holds four nutlets each containing a seed

Part of the mint family, the Archangel resembles a stinging nettle but its pretty golden flowers belie its true nature. It grows in abundance in dense patches of woodland, quite often amongst Bluebells, stealing their glory as they begin to die. A spring bloom, it was once thought to keep evil spirits and spells at bay, and also to protect cattle. Growing no more than around 28 cm (11 in) high, this bloom has bright yellow lips, with reddish brown markings inside that guide pollinators to its crop of nectar.

Ragwort

Jacobaea vulgaris

FAMILY NAME Asteraceae

CHARACTERISTICS A tall plant growing up to 91.4 cm (36 in), it has a basal rosette of toothed leaves and a cluster of yellow, daisy-like flowers

HABITAT Waste ground, pastures, paddocks and natural areas near the coast

DISTRIBUTION Native to Europe, North Africa and western Asia

FLOWERS AND FRUIT Flowers come in flat-headed clusters that can be seen summer to late autumn, seeds are attached to a feathery pappus

While it's considered a weed and is highly toxic to any livestock that graze upon it, this pretty plant is a favourite of bees and the striking Cinnabar moth. It's also known as Stinking Willie, partly because of its pungent aroma, and also because it supposedly spread in the path of William, Duke of Cumberland, during the battle of Culloden. One of its earliest titles was Staggerwort, which refers to the ungainly gait of one who has succumbed to its poison. The famous herbalist Culpepper favoured its charms as a treatment for what he termed 'old and filthy ulcers of the privities'.

Spear Thistle

Cirsium vulgare

FAMILY NAME Asteraceae

CHARACTERISTICS Grows up to 1.5 m (5 ft) in height, with lanceolate leaves, pinnately lobed and sharply spined; it has purple fluffy-looking flowers

HABITAT Pastures, roadside verges, field edges

DISTRIBUTION Found on every continent except Antarctica

FLOWERS AND FRUIT The flowers sit on top of a spiny ball and the fruit is a one-seeded tufted achene

While it may look weed-like, this common thistle bears bright pink to mauve florets and is a food source for a variety of wildlife. Birds like the delicate Goldfinch seek it out, and its nectar is a popular draw for a range of colourful butterflies, including the Small Copper and the Monarch. An edible snack for humans too; the stems can be peeled and boiled, and the taproots eaten raw in salads. This plant is also known as the Bull Thistle and the Scots or Scottish Thistle.

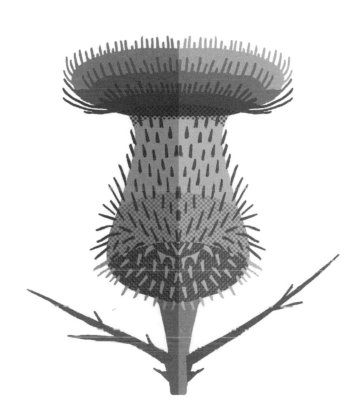

Common Spotted Orchid

Dactylorhiza fuchsii

FAMILY NAME Orchidaceae

CHARACTERISTICS A short to medium height perennial with lance-like leaves
that have purple oval-shaped spots; flowers cluster together

HABITAT Damp grassland, marshes, fens, scrub, hedgerows and open woodland

DISTRIBUTION Widespread across Europe, also found extending eastward into
Siberia, Mongolia and Xinjiang

FLOWERS AND FRUIT The flowers, which bloom in summer, range in colour
from white, pale pink to purplish in hue; they have three-lobed lips, daubed with
darker stripes and spots

This beautiful bloom has sweetly scented flowers that form
cone-like clusters along a central spike. The heady aroma is
particularly attractive to day-flying moths, and the array of
colours, from soft candy pinks to darker purple hues, make it
a joy to witness during the summer months. It's been given an
assortment of titles, from Adam and Eve to Crow-Foot and the
even more gruesome Dead Man's Finger – a reference to the
protruding stems that burst from the earth to greet the sun.

Edelweiss

Leontopodium nivale

FAMILY NAME Asteraceae

CHARACTERISTICS A perennial plant with lance-shaped, woolly white leaves and yellow flower heads

HABITAT Alpine pastures, in rocky crevices and outcrops

DISTRIBUTION It has a distribution that extends along the highest areas of Europe and Asia

FLOWERS AND FRUIT The leaves are snowy white and are often mistaken for the bloom, but the flower itself is tiny, yellowish in colour and short-lived, meaning the plant produces fewer over time

This hardy plant manages to thrive in some of the trickiest terrains thanks to its fibrous root system, which helps it cling firmly to the rocky slopes it favours. With an abundance of woolly white hairs, the thick leaves provide a barrier against the wind and rain and also retain moisture. Its name in German means 'noble', which is fitting should you catch a glimpse of it growing, against the odds, in the wild.

Rosebay Willowherb

Chamaenerion angustifolium

FAMILY NAME Onagraceae

CHARACTERISTICS An upright perennial with lance-shaped leaves arranged in spiral formations lining the stem; it has tall spires of pink flowers

HABITAT Woodland clearings, waste ground, roadsides, beside tracks

DISTRIBUTION Native to the UK but widely distributed around the world including Europe and North America

FLOWERS AND FRUIT The pinkish purple flowers have dark purple sepals, the fruit is a pink to purple capsule, which splits to release the seeds

Named because the leaves resemble that of the willow plant, this striking wildflower has tall stalks with plumes of large pink flowers and a staircase of leaves around the stem. It's adept at spreading and colonising new areas, mainly because the seeds have tiny parachutes, helping them to glide upon the breeze and go further afield. It's also known as Fireweed, because the heat from fires and bonfires provides a helping hand during the germination process.

Lady's Bedstraw

Galium verum

FAMILY NAME Rubiaceae

CHARACTERISTICS This flowering plant has angular stems, with small, narrow leaves in whorls and soft clusters of bright yellow blooms

HABITAT Grasslands, meadows, pastures, moorland, dunes

DISTRIBUTION Found across most of Europe, North Africa and temperate Asia

FLOWERS AND FRUIT Tiny, four-petalled yellow flowers that bloom from summer through to early autumn

This sprawling downy perennial carpets the ground in frothy golden sunshine and can be seen on patches of dry grassland and wetter terrain, by the sea. With its sweet scent of freshly mown hay and honey, it's a pleasure to all the senses, and if gathered in its purest form then dried, it can be used to fragrance a room. Medieval legend suggests that the Virgin Mary lay on a bed of Lady's Bedstraw when she gave birth to the baby Jesus. As such, the plant is often stuffed into mattresses to ease labour pains.

California Poppy

Eschscholzia californica

FAMILY NAME Papaveraceae

CHARACTERISTICS A popular perennial with feathery greenish-grey
foliage and silky orange to yellow flowers

HABITAT Coastal dunes and scrubs, dry plains and prairies

DISTRIBUTION Native to the southwestern United States and northern
Mexico and naturalised in southern Europe, Asia and Australia

FLOWERS AND FRUIT The four-petalled flowers are solitary and have a
deep orange spot at the base, the bloom produces narrow capsule-like fruits

Although a perennial, this plant is often grown as an annual.
It usually begins its sunshine reign early spring and can
bloom through till early autumn in the right conditions. Its
bright golden hue makes it the ideal choice to be the flower
of the Golden State, a mantel it commandeered in 1903.
Also known as the Corn, or Golden Poppy, its beautiful
blooms have long been associated with the sleep of the dead,
although this is likely because the unripe seed pods are a
source of opium.

Winter Cress

Barbarea vulgaris

FAMILY NAME Brassicaceae

CHARACTERISTICS This plant has branched flower stems with small deeply-lobed leaves, the flowers are bright yellow

HABITAT Damp meadows and ditches, riverbanks, roadsides, hedges and waste ground

DISTRIBUTION Native to Europe, Asia and North Africa, it has been naturalised in North America and New Zealand

FLOWERS AND FRUIT The blooms form delicate, bright yellow clusters at the end of the stem; the fruits, known as siliques, are long narrow capsules containing many seeds

This eye-catching herbaceous plant belongs to the mustard family, and is an edible favourite often used to brighten salads. It flowers from spring through to mid-summer, in a glorious profusion of sunshine yellow. Also known as Bittercress, Indian Posey and Yellow Rocket, it's thought to have anti-carcinogenic properties and was favoured by the Cherokee Indians, who brewed it up as a medicinal tea to purify the blood. In Europe, they used the leaves in folk remedies and poultices to heal wounds.

Alpine Snowbell

Soldanella alpina

FAMILY NAME Primulaceae

CHARACTERISTICS A perennial with small, rounded leathery
leaves and bell-shaped nodding flowers, usually purple in hue

HABITAT High mountains, woods, damp pastures and rocky terrain

DISTRIBUTION Native to the Alps and the Pyrenees

FLOWERS AND FRUIT Bright violet flowers with petals that flare
outward and are fringed along the edges; the fruit is capsule shaped

These lovely evergreens form in clumps, adding dots of
brightness to the loftiest of vistas. Also known as Blue
Moonwort, this delicate looking bloom appears at the first
sign of snow melt in its native environment after spending
many months covered in an icy white blanket – a sure
sign, if one were needed, of its a hardy character. Alpine
Snowbells herald the coming of spring and are seen as a
positive omen. Today it is cultivated around the world and
is a popular addition to rock gardens and alpine beds.

Wild Tulip

Tulipa sylvestris

FAMILY NAME Liliaceae

CHARACTERISTICS A medium-sized plant, with a slender, upright stem that grows from a bulb and produces a single yellow flower

HABITAT Dry grasslands, meadows and woodland

DISTRIBUTION Originates in Europe and North Africa but has now spread through several continents

FLOWERS AND FRUIT It has star-shaped bright yellow blooms with six pointed petals; the fruit is a capsule that splits to release two or three seeds

This vibrant, vigorous wildflower is commonly seen bathing woodland in its golden glow in mid to late spring. Also known as the Botanical Tulip and the Rock Garden Tulip because of its ability to grow in all environments; its uplifting lemony scent is a gift of nature. The Wild Tulip is often seen growing together in tight clumps, which makes the plant appear to have more than one flower. The nodding blooms lose their reddish orange tint to the backs of the petals as they open fully to the light.

Dog Tooth Violet

Erythronium dens-canis

FAMILY NAME Liliaceae

CHARACTERISTICS A clump-forming bulbous perennial with drooping, lily-like pink flowers, usually one to each stem

HABITAT Shady, damp woodlands and forests

DISTRIBUTION Originates from Europe and Asia

FLOWERS AND FRUIT The mauve flowers have reflexed tepals with yellow and red zones at the base; the fruit is a seed pod

This delicate bloom, which varies in colour from pale lilac to a deeper purplish-pink, comes to life at the beginning of spring. The leaves are striking, too, and marbled with deep brown spots, making this an easy shrub to spot during woodland walks. Grouped together in shady spots, the flowers can grow between 10–30.5 cm (4–12 in) high depending on the moisture of the soil. A favourite with gardeners, it's often used to brighten borders or rockeries near ponds and streams.

Elderflower Orchid

Dactylorhiza sambucina

FAMILY NAME Orchidaceae

CHARACTERISTICS A tuberous flowering perennial, short and stumpy, with lance shaped leaves that are often purple spotted

HABITAT Pastures, grassland, coppices and mountain meadows

DISTRIBUTION Found in Finland, Sweden and Norway, and as far as southern France; also grows in some central European countries

FLOWERS AND FRUIT The large flowers are either purply red or yellow; the fruit is capsule shaped, containing dust-like seeds

This striking flower gets its name from the similarity it bears to the Black Elderberry and was often confused with this species because the two plants grew together on mountain meadows. This plant has a clever trick of fooling inexperienced bees into pollinating its blooms for no reward; in reality, the flower has no nectar or pollen to gather, so it's a futile task. While the red and yellow blooms appear together, the red tends to blossom first, with flowers emerging from mid-spring to early summer.

Pink Sorrel

Oxalis articulata

FAMILY NAME Oxalidaceae

CHARACTERISTICS A short, hairy perennial, with three-lobed leaves, heart shaped and daubed with orange or brown dots, the pink flowers grow in clusters

HABITAT Waste ground, gardens, meadows and by the seashore

DISTRIBUTION Native to South America, this plant is widespread throughout Europe

FLOWERS AND FRUIT The pale to dark pink flowers bloom from mid-spring to early autumn; the fruit is a fleshy capsule that releases seeds when ripe

This stemless perennial is a hardy deciduous plant with an array of pretty flowers, which often remain hidden beneath the clover-like leaves. The sun, too, has an effect on the blooms, making them curl up into a tube, but positioned in light they will open fully to absorb the rays. Although it's often considered a weed, it's sought after by gardeners as a natural bedding plant – this is thanks to the way it spreads through its rhizomes and inhibits the growth of other weeds.

Evening Primrose

Oenothera biennis

FAMILY NAME Onagraceae

CHARACTERISTICS A biennial bush-like plant, with a hairy stem and large yellow flowers

HABITAT Fields, clearings, dry sandy ground and roadsides

DISTRIBUTION Native to eastern and central North America, but has naturalised in temperate and subtropical regions around the world

FLOWERS AND FRUIT The flowers are large goblet-like blooms with four petals, the fruits are capsules with around 100 seeds inside

Also known as the Yellow Primrose, King's Cure All and the Fever Plant, the Evening Primrose is renowned for its healing properties. The prize ingredient comes from the seed oil, which has been used throughout Europe in medications since the 1600s. All parts of the plant, including the roots, were favoured by several Native American tribes, who used it as a food source. It's thought that the genus name comes from the two Greek words *oinos* and *theras* meaning 'wine seeker', a nod to the original use of plant roots in scenting wine.

Blue Phlox

Phlox divaricata

FAMILY NAME Polemoniaceae

CHARACTERISTICS A semi-evergreen perennial with loose clusters of blue to lilac flowers, which sit at the tip of a hairy, sticky stem

HABITAT Moist deciduous woodlands, forests and wetlands

DISTRIBUTION Native to North America, from Canada to Florida

FLOWERS AND FRUIT This plants blooms in late spring to early summer; the flowers are swiftly followed by rounded greenish fruits that eventually turn into brown ovoid seed capsules

This pretty wildflower, also known as Wild Blue Phlox and Wild Sweet William, seeks out dappled patches of woodland shade to flourish in dense clumps. The tubular flowers have five petals, and come in a range of shades, from white and palest blue to violet, lavender and pink. Its fragrant sweetness makes it a favourite of long-tongued pollinators, including butterflies such as Tiger Swallowtails, Skippers, Sphinx Moths and Bumblebees. The word 'Phlox' comes from the Greek word for flame, which refers to the way it sweeps colour through the forest floor.

Dog Rose

Rosa canina

FAMILY NAME Rosaceae

CHARACTERISTICS Deciduous or semi evergreen shrub, with strong hooked thorns and pinnate leaves; flowers are large and pale to deep pink in hue

HABITAT Scrubland, hedgerows and woodland edges

DISTRIBUTION Native to Europe, northwest Africa and western Asia, an invasive species in Australia and New Zealand

FLOWERS AND FRUIT The pretty blooms flower during spring and summer; the fruits are red berry-like hips that appear in clusters and ripen in the autumn

With a faint aroma of sweetness to match the delicate petals of each flower, the Dog Rose could be considered a gentle beauty – but do not be fooled. The sharp spiny thorns are one reason for the name as they resemble canine teeth; the other was the popular belief that the roots could cure the bite of a rabid dog. In Medieval times this bloom was placed at the end of a maiden's bed to express the King's carnal interest. Once received, the girl would slip undetected into the King's chambers while the rest of the court slept.

Alpine Poppy

Papaver alpinum

FAMILY NAME Papaveraceae

CHARACTERISTICS A short, hairy perennial, with leaves that form a rosette close to the ground; flowers are saucer shaped and come in a range of hues

HABITAT Rocky, mountainous, and snowy slopes

DISTRIBUTION Native to Europe, it thrives in cold winters and at high elevations and can be found in Alaska and the Rocky Mountain region

FLOWERS AND FRUIT The cup-shaped flowers bloom in the summer and can be orange, yellow, red or white; fruit is a bristled capsule containing seeds

In sharp contrast to the harsh terrain where it flourishes, the Alpine Poppy is a bloom that proves the point that beauty can thrive anywhere. Also known as Rooted Poppies or Artic Poppies, these cool weather favourites have fern-like leaves and delicate papery flowers with four large petals. They generally bloom in summer, but the leaves also display their bright jewel green splendour in warmer months.

Dyer's Greenweed

Genista tinctoria

FAMILY NAME Fabaceae

CHARACTERISTICS A deciduous shrubby plant, with greyish leaves that are oval to linear lanceolate; the flowers grow on leafy stalked spikes

HABITAT Grassy meadows, pastures, heaths, field margins and road verges

DISTRIBUTION Native to Europe and western Asia, it is cultivated around the world

FLOWERS AND FRUIT Vibrant yellow pea-like blooms that appear during spring and summer; the fruit is a long hairless seed pod, which ripens as the seeds mature

Also known as Dyer's Whin, Waxen Woad and Waxen Wood, this vivid golden bloom was used in ancient times to produce yellow dye. When combined with woad it would turn green. The Latin name *tinctoria* means 'used as dye', another reference to its original purpose. A member of the pea family, Dyer's Greenweed is a popular medicinal plant and the powdered seeds can be administered as a mild purgative. It was also used in folk medicine as a tincture for dropsy, gout and rheumatism.

Ragged Robin

Lychnis flos-cuculi

FAMILY NAME Caryophyllaceae

CHARACTERISTICS A hardy perennial, bushy, with lanceolate leaves and loose clusters of raggedy pink flowers

HABITAT Marshes, fens, damp pastures and woods

DISTRIBUTION Found growing naturally in Europe, Caucasus and Siberia

FLOWERS AND FRUIT Bright pink flowers with five petals that are deeply lobed to give a torn, tattered appearance; the fruits are small capsules packed with an abundance of seeds

A distinctive looking wildflower because of its straggly appearance, the Ragged Robin is steeped in folklore. In the language of flowers it's associated with wit and ardour, but it was also considered unlucky to pick the bloom and take it into your home. That said, gentlemen in times gone by were urged to carry the flower in their pocket. If it survived for more than a few days, then any romantic endeavours would be blessed and true love would flourish. A remedy made from this plant was used in folk medicine to cure snake bites.

Foxglove

Digitalis purpurea

FAMILY NAME Plantaginaceae

CHARACTERISTICS Fluted pink to purple flowers on a spike that can grow up to 1.5 m (5 ft) in height

HABITAT Woodland hedgerows, gardens, heathland, roadside verges

DISTRIBUTION Native to Europe, western Asia and northwest Africa

FLOWERS AND FRUIT Tube-shaped flowers, pinkish purple in hue with darker coloured spots on the lower lip; fruit is a seed-filled capsule that changes from green to black when ripe

A favourite with pollinators, particularly longer-tongued bees; the bright bloom draws them in, and the lower lip makes the perfect landing spot from which they can crawl up the tube. In folklore the Foxglove has a reputation for being able to kill or cure. Also known as Goblin Gloves, it's no surprise that this enchanting flower is associated with fairies, who were thought to seek sanctuary in the flower head. The finger-shaped bloom was also considered the glove of choice for foxes, who covered their paws with the petals to silence their movements.

Poet's Daffodil

Narcissus poeticus

FAMILY NAME Amaryllidaceae

CHARACTERISTICS This bloom has linear leaf blades, which grow at the base of the plant; flowers have pure white petals that surround a yellow cup, fringed with red

HABITAT Fields, roadsides, lawn edges

DISTRIBUTION Found in central and southern Europe, and has spread to other temperate regions

FLOWERS AND FRUIT Blooms mid to late spring; the solitary white flower has recurved perianth segments and a yellow inner cup

Also known as Pheasant's Eye Daffodil, this stunning herbaceous perennial has a red-fringed corona and a gorgeous, sweet scent to complement its beauty. One of the first daffodils to be cultivated, this bloom is linked to the Greek myth of Narcissus, the son of the river god Cephissus. He was so vain that as punishment the goddess Nemesis made him fall in love with himself; the resulting disillusionment caused him to commit suicide. The glorious flowers sprang forth where he fell.

Snowdrop

Galanthus

FAMILY NAME Amaryllidaceae

CHARACTERISTICS Pure white bell-shaped blooms at the end of a stalk, they grow up to 15 cm (6 in) tall

HABITAT Woodland, along riverbanks, in parks, meadows, gardens and scrub

DISTRIBUTION Widespread throughout Europe

FLOWERS AND FRUIT Flowers are made up of six tepals, which are petal-like segments with three inner tepals that display a green 'v' shaped pattern; the fruit is a spherical capsule that contains brown seeds

A common winter bloom, this delicate flower can be seen growing in clumps in the first couple of months of the year. A sure sign that spring is on its way, the appearance of snowdrops is considered auspicious, making this flower a symbol of hope around the world. That said, if you were to chance upon a solitary bloom it was thought to be an ill omen. Traditionally used in medicine for pain relief, more recently scientists have discovered that a compound from the bulb helps to alleviate symptoms of dementia.

Spotter's Guide

This checklist will give you the basics you need to identify flowers, plants and herbs growing in the wild. You'll know where to look, and the highlighted points will help you distinguish between the different types listed in this book. Along with this handy guide, keep a pen and notebook with you, so that you can mark down your finds and even make sketches if you're feeling artistic!

☐ **Blue Iris**
Iris spuria (p9)

☐ **Rock Rose**
Cistus (p10)

☐ **Cornflower**
Centaurea cyanus (p13)

☐ **Italian Buckthorn**
Rhamnus alaternus (p14)

88

□ **Common Daisy**
Bellis perennis (p17)

□ **Cowslip**
Primula veris (p18)

□ **Meadow Saxifrage**
Saxifraga granulata (p21)

□ **Creeping Buttercup**
Ranunculus repens (p22)

□ **Bluebell**
Hyacinthoides (p25)

□ **Yarrow**
Achillea millefolium (p26)

☐ **Dandelion**

Taraxacum (p29)

☐ **Common Dog Violet**

Viola riviniana (p30)

☐ **Solomon's Seal**

Polygonatum (p33)

☐ **Red Campion**

Silene dioica (p34)

☐ **Yellow Wort**

Blackstonia perfoliata (p37)

☐ **Red Clover**

Trifolium pratense (p38)

□ **Autumn Crocus**
Colchicum autumnale (p41)

□ **Yellow Archangel**
Lamium galeobdolon (p42)

□ **Ragwort**
Jacobaea vulgaris (p45)

□ **Spear Thistle**
Cirsium vulgare (p46)

□ **Common Spotted Orchid**
Dactylorhiza fuchsii (p49)

□ **Edelweiss**
Leontopodium nivale (p50)

☐ **Rosebay Willowherb**

Chamaenerion angustifolium (p53)

☐ **Lady's Bedstraw**

Galium verum (p54)

☐ **California Poppy**

Eschscholzia californica (p57)

☐ **Winter Cress**

Barbarea vulgaris (p58)

☐ **Alpine Snowbell**

Soldanella alpina (p61)

☐ **Wild Tulip**

Tulipa sylvestris (p62)

☐ **Dog Tooth Violet**
Erythronium dens-canis (p65)

☐ **Elderflower Orchid**
Dactylorhiza sambucina (p66)

☐ **Pink Sorrel**
Oxalis articulata (p69)

☐ **Evening Primrose**
Oenothera biennis (p70)

☐ **Blue Phlox**
Phlox divaricata (p73)

☐ **Dog Rose**
Rosa canina (p74)

☐ **Alpine Poppy**

Papaver alpinum (p77)

☐ **Dyer's Greenweed**

Genista tinctoria (p78)

☐ **Ragged Robin**

Lychnis flos-cuculi (p81)

☐ **Foxglove**

Digitalis purpurea (p82)

☐ **Poet's Daffodil**

Narcissus poeticus (p85)

☐ **Snowdrop**

Galanthus (p86)

TOM FROST
Print Maker

Print maker and illustrator Tom Frost graduated from
Falmouth College of Arts in 2001, returning to his home
town of Bristol to work as an illustrator for a number
of years. He now divides his time between printmaking,
restoring his crumbling Georgian house in rural Wales
and raising a young family. In recent years he has worked
with clients including the V&A, Perry's Cider, Art Angels,
Freight Household Goods, *Selvedge* magazine, Betty &
Dupree, The Archivist and Yorkshire Sculpture Park. His
work highlights a fascination for old matchboxes, stamps,
folk art, tin toys, children's books and the natural world.

MANAGING DIRECTOR Sarah Lavelle
SENIOR COMMISSIONING EDITOR
Harriet Butt
ASSISTANT EDITOR Oreolu Grillo
SERIES DESIGNER Emily Lapworth
DESIGNER Alicia House
ILLUSTRATOR Tom Frost
WORDS Alison Davies
SENIOR PRODUCTION CONTROLLER
Sabeena Atchia

Published in 2023 by Quadrille, an imprint
of Hardie Grant Publishing

Quadrille
52–54 Southwark Street
London SE1 1UN
quadrille.com

Text, design and layout © 2023 Quadrille
Illustrations © 2023 Tom Frost

Cataloguing in Publication Data:
a catalogue record for this book is
available from the British Library.

ISBN 978 1 78713 958 9
Printed in China